INDIAN ART
AND THE ART OF CEYLON,
CENTRAL AND SOUTH-EAST ASIA

INDIAN ART
AND THE ART OF CEYLON,
CENTRAL AND SOUTH-EAST ASIA

General editor
Francesco Abbate

Translated by
Jean Richardson

Octopus Books
London · New York · Sydney · Hong Kong

English version first published 1972 by
Octopus Books Limited
59 Grosvenor Street, London W1
Translation © 1972 Octopus Books Limited

Distributed in Australia by
Angus & Robertson (Publishers) Pty Ltd
102 Glover Street, Cremorne, Sydney

ISBN 7064 0061 5

Originally published in Italian by
Fratelli Fabbri Editore
© 1966 Fratelli Fabbri Editore, Milan

Printed in Italy by Fratelli Fabbri Editore

CONTENTS

India	7
Ceylon	137
Afghanistan	139
Nepal and Tibet	147
Siam and Burma	149
Cambodia and Vietnam	150
Indonesia	152
Chronological Table	153
Bibliography	154
Index of Illustrations	155

INDIA

Protected in the north by the peaks of the Himalayas and lapped in the south by the Indian ocean, India covers an area equal to Europe (excluding Russia). In the interior, arid desert zones alternate with fertile monsoon regions, jungle, plateaux and sunny valleys crossed by great rivers. Over the centuries many peoples have entered this vast land and settled in it for varying periods. Aryans, Persians, Greeks and Moslems have each added something of their civilization to the original native elements of Indian culture and society. Inevitably a many-sided civilization, the source of a rich and varied art, has sprung from such a mixture of surroundings and peoples.

For a long time Indian art has been the least known of the oriental arts. This is perhaps because of a lack of evidence from the earliest periods and because, from a western point of view, it is difficult to understand the spirit which has governed all Indian art and which is so different from the spirit of the west. It is at once ascetic and sensual, both celebrating and denying the individual's love of life and combining free instinct with rigid reason. The fact that such contrasting elements can be found side by side in Indian art is explained by the culturally mixed conditions we have already mentioned. If we add to this the constant religious exaltation which has been part of Indian civilization since its beginnings and an extensive use of symbolism, we have the basic elements of an art which, in little more than the last century, has become of great interest to the western world.

The first evidence of civilization in India dates from about the third millennium BC. The life of the people, as in Mesopotamia, was based on agriculture. Small statues of the Mother Goddess show that their religion had contacts with the Mesopotamian and Mediterranean worlds. The most important culture was that of the Indus Valley, which lasted into the second millennium and had its main centres at Harappa and Mohenjo-daro. The social structure was organized into classes and dominated by a caste of priests. Their art was linked either to their religious worship or to the practical necessities of life, as we can see from the various kinds of pottery, weapons, jewellery, images of the deity and the few architectural remains that have survived. The steatite seals form a group apart. They are usually rectangular, more rarely cylindrical or round, and bear inscriptions in a language which has not yet been deciphered, together with various images, often of animals such as oxen, bulls, elephants, tigers and rhinoceroses.

These are sometimes accompanied by images of gods or mythical heroes, but while the animals look natural and full of life, the human figures seem curiously stiff and conventional. (The same difference can also be seen in ceramic decoration.)

One of the greatest mysteries of India concerns the art of the civilization that occurred between about 1400 BC and the beginning of the Christian era. Nothing, or almost nothing of it remains, but it is hard to believe that during a period having such a wealth of literature there were no visual arts. The most probable reason for this lack of evidence is that the artists worked almost exclusively in perishable materials such as wood and terracotta, which in India were more plentiful even than stone. In the fifteenth century BC the Aryans, a semi-nomadic people from the interior of Asia, occupied nearly the whole of India, overwhelming the local population by their advanced methods of warfare and the speed of their horses. The Aryan period is thought to extend from 1400 BC–AD 750, that is, until the rise of the Medieval Hindu phase. During this period India saw a succession of rulers, the introduction of various religions and the gradual development of a mature art that became the classical art of the Gupta period (AD 320–530). But there is hardly any evidence of this development before, at the earliest, the second century BC. The sacred books, the Vedas, and the two great heroic epics, the *Mahabharata* and the *Ramayana*, belong to this Aryan period. They form the basis of the main Indian religions including

1 *Indus Valley art : Large jar (2500–1500 BC)*. *National Museum, New Delhi.*

2   *Indus Valley art : Seal with bull (2500–1500 BC).*
National Museum, Karachi.

3 Indian art (Mauryan period) : Statuette of the Mother Goddess in grey terracotta (c. 2nd century BC). Prince of Wales Museum, Bombay.

1   Indus Valley art: *Large jar* (2500–1500 BC). National Museum, New Delhi.
Indus Valley pottery consisted largely of storage vessels that were covered with a red-ochre slip and decorated with abstract motifs – often circles and leaf patterns.

2   Indus Valley art: *Seal with bull* (2500–1500 BC). National Museum, Karachi.
Numerous seals have survived from the Indus Valley period, generally rectangular in shape and bearing emblems of divinities and animals, commonly the bull.

3   Indian art (Mauryan period): *Statuette of the Mother Goddess in grey terracotta (c.* 2nd century BC). Prince of Wales Museum, Bombay.
The Mauryan period marks a significant step forward in Indian art, which became more realistic and more assured; at the same time statues of the Mother Goddess persisted and retained their prehistoric characteristics of shape and appliqué technique.

4   Indian art (Mauryan period): *Capital of an Asoka column* (3rd century BC). Museum of Indian Art, Calcutta.
King Asoka erected tall columns at his city gates and outside temples. The shafts are typically plain and smooth but the capitals are richly decorated with a stylized lotus flower shape crowned by the figure of an animal.

5, 6, 7   Indian art (Sunga period): *Details from the railing of the Stupa of Bharhut* (2nd century BC). Museum of Indian Art, Calcutta.
Only the outermost railing (*vedika*) of the Stupa of Bharhut remains. Once it enclosed the centre of the stupa itself, and it is decorated with figures supporting the pillars. The central part of the *vedika* consists of pillars and medallions decorated with reliefs of narrative scenes or motifs based on haloes and lotus flowers.

4   *Indian art (Mauryan period) : Capital of an Asoka column (3rd century BC). Museum of Indian Art, Calcutta.*

15

Buddhism and Jainism. In addition, a series of foreign invaders, including the Persians and the armies led by Alexander the Great, made their contribution to the growth of Indian civilization.

There were many small kingdoms in India towards the middle of the first millennium BC; one of these, the Maurya, overpowered the others and by a succession of conquests formed the first united kingdom in India. The most famous Mauryan king was Asoka (d. 232 BC), who is best known for his great effort to promote Buddhism. The oldest artistic records, which date from after the Aryan invasion, belong to his reign. He also built a large number of stupas, the sacred Buddhist burial monuments, and at the entrance to cities and along the roadside he erected great columns crowned with the figures of animals and decorated at the base with Buddhist religious symbols. During his reign stone gradually replaced wood for building, and the history of Indian art really begins with the appearance of these early stone monuments.

Many of the stupas built by Asoka have been destroyed or altered in later periods, but the architectural concept remained the same, and we shall now try to explain it. The stupa consists of a stone hemisphere representing the universe, raised on one or more platforms and crowned by a series of umbrellas signifying the vault of the heavens. The holy ground outside is enclosed by a stone railing of pillars with four gates, or *toranas*, decorated with various reliefs. Basically the stupa is a development of the ancient

7 *Indian art (Sunga period) : The railing of the Stupa of Bharhut (2nd century BC). Museum of Indian Art, Calcutta.*

burial monuments of the Aryan rulers. Asoka was also responsible for the first Buddhist retreats (*viharas*), which included cells for the monks, a refectory and a vaulted preaching hall or *chaitya*.

Among the most famous early stupas were those at Bharhut and Sanchi, built by Asoka but later enlarged and modified when, on his death, the Mauryas were succeeded by the Sunga dynasty. The railing, gates, pillars and many bas-reliefs from the Stupa of Bharhut have survived, and most of them are now in Calcutta Museum. They portray a wide variety of scenes and decorative motifs, and although the technique is still rather crude it is also lively and effective. During the first centuries of Buddhism the figure of Buddha was never portrayed. Instead, he was alluded to through such images as footprints, the lotus flower, the wheel of the law and other symbols. In the decorative reliefs of the stupa these images are combined with a host of minor deities, nymphs and heavenly spirits, mythical creatures drawn from fairy stories or from the oldest popular traditions, which were adapted to Buddhist mythology. There is also a mass of plants and flowers depicted with a transparent love of nature. The art of Bharhut has a bursting vitality, it is natural, fresh and distinguished by the simple enthusiasm with which the artists saw and portrayed the world around them.

The same can be said of the Stupa of Sanchi, which is the work of a number of periods but contrives to be a masterpiece of architectural and sculptural harmony. In a remarkable way its creators have

8   *Indian art (Sunga period) : Bust of a yakshi from Bharhut*
(2nd century BC). Museum of Fine Arts, Boston.

9   *Indian art (Satavahana period) : Detail of the North gate of the Great Stupa at Sanchi (1st century BC).*

10   *Indian art (Satavahana period) : Detail of the West gate of the Great Stupa at Sanchi (1st century BC).*

11 *Indian art (Satavahana period) : Detail of the East gate of the Great Stupa at Sanchi (1st century BC).*

8   Indian art (Sunga period): *Bust of a yakshi from Bharhut* (2nd century BC). Museum of Fine Arts, Boston. The many figures of yakshis, or tree-nymphs, belong historically to an earlier nature cult which was later allowed to survive alongside the Buddhist faith – probably because of its great popular appeal.

9   Indian art (Satavahana period): *Detail of the North gate of the Great Stupa at Sanchi* (1st century BC).
The north is the best preserved of the four gateways of Stupa No. 1 at Sanchi. The three very ornate crossbeams portray episodes in the life of Buddha and stories of the princes.

10   Indian art (Satavahana period): *Detail of the West gate of the Great Stupa at Sanchi* (1st century BC).
On the three crossbeams, supported by strange capitals with grotesque, corpulent dwarfs, is a crowded assortment of battle-scenes and myths.

12   *Indian art (Sunga period) : View at Sanchi of Stupa No. 1 or the Great Stupa, and Stupa No. 3 (2nd century BC).*

11   Indian art (Satavahana period): *Detail of the East gate of the Great Stupa at Sanchi* (1st century BC).
The sculptures of the gateways at Sanchi show, even at this early date, great confidence in the blending of sensual and spiritual elements.

12   Indian art (Sunga period): *View at Sanchi of Stupa No. 1 or the Great Stupa and Stupa No. 3* (2nd century BC).
During the Mauryan dynasty and its immediate successors the stupa was almost a hemisphere, but later it was elongated and became very slender.

13   Indian art (Sunga period): *Stupa No. 3 at Sanchi* (2nd century BC).
The decoration of the stupa itself is very restrained: the railings that surround it bear no sculptural decoration, which is applied only to the great gateways.

13   *Indian art (Sunga period) : Stupa No. 3 at Sanchi (2nd century BC).*

recaptured in stone the decorative effect of woodwork and have concealed the function of the columns and pillars under a riot of ornamental reliefs. The sculpture of Sanchi is more mature than that of Bharhut, but it reflects the same ingenuous and optimistic view of life. It reveals a renewed sense of security and faith in nature after the threatening forces of evil have finally been vanquished by Buddha.

In the second century AD the Sunga dynasty was overcome by the Satavahanas from the Deccan, who shortly succeeded in controlling a large part of India. The Satavahana period is considered to be one of the happiest and most splendid phases of early Indian art, and it was then that the four superb gateways were added to the stupa at Sanchi and the first Buddhist caves were built in the Deccan. These were originally very bare and simple, but eventually they acquired many fine paintings and sculpture. The caves of Ajanta, which were later famous for their frescoes, date from this period. Very elaborate columns and pillars ornamented with animal figures were introduced into the monasteries, and the entrances were decorated with fantastic reliefs of lotus flowers and smiling heavenly nymphs.

In the first century of the Christian era the Satavahana moved their capital to the eastern shores where they built a number of stupas including the famous one at Amaravati. Reliefs dating from the first century AD have survived, and they depict episodes in the life of Buddha such his miracles and mystical experiences. He is now shown in human form, surrounded by a crowd of spirits, nymphs and other characters. The balanced composition of the scenes reveals a knowledge of Graeco-Roman art, and this is further confirmed by the treatment of individual figures. The later reliefs, dating from the second century AD, show a rapid development in style, and the elegant, elongated figures with their softness and grace are the greatest achievement of Satavahana art.

At the same time that Satavahana art was reaching its peak in the sculptures of Amaravati, many other artistic centres were flourishing in India. The Megavahana dynasty founded a kingdom in Orissa (ancient Kalinga) and traces of it remain in some cave-temples dedicated to the Jain religion. Even more interesting in this period are various artistic events in the north-west regions, where there was a constant interchange of civilizations and cultures. The Indians in the north-west felt the influence of provincial Roman and late Greek civilizations, which reached them across the borders of Turkestan and northern Afghanistan, and these elements were fused with others drawn from Scythian tribes. Finally, in the first century AD, the Kushans, a tribe of nomads from central Asia, founded a kingdom that included a large area of northern and central India.

They did not have their own tradition of art and civilization, and so they adopted the Hellenistic one which they introduced into India. The artistic activity of this period reveals a surprising assortment of motifs and characteristics. There are delicate gold objects

14 *Indian art (Satavahana period) : Relief from the cave-temple at Karle (end of 1st century BC).*

14   Indian art (Satavahana period): *Relief from the cave-temple at Karle* (end of 1st century BC).
The main figures are designed in a controlled, frontal style, and the treatment of the clothes, hair-styles and jewels adds to their monumentality.

15   Indian art (Satavahana period): *The cave-temple at Karle* (end of 1st century BC – beginning of 2nd century AD).
The structure of the cave-temple of Karle is highly complex. It has a massive façade screen of carved stone and the interior measures 124 x 46 feet.

16   Indian art (Satavahana period): *Entrance to the cave-temple at Bhaja, near Bombay* (1st century BC – 1st century AD).
The rock-cut temple of Bhaja consisted of a long chaitya-hall supported by a continuous row of plain octagonal columns; the façade was originally timbered.

15   16

17   Indian art (Satavahana period): *Marble reliefs from the Stupa of Amaravati* (1st–2nd century AD). British Museum, London.

The Great Stupa of Amaravati was covered with magnificent decorations depicting scenes from the life of Buddha.

18   Indian art (Satavahana period): *Carved panel showing the Stupa of Amaravati*. British Museum, London.

The Stupa of Amaravati, begun about the 2nd century BC and considerably enlarged and embellished in the 1st and 2nd centuries AD, suffered badly from a succession of local rulers. Excavations have since restored many of its panels.

19   Indian art (Satavahana period): *Reliefs from the Stupa of Amaravati* (1st–2nd century AD). (*Above*) National Museum, Madras. (*Below*) British Museum, London.

The limestone carvings at Amaravati portray densely crowded groups of men and animals and are executed with great exuberance and a feeling of nervous tension.

17   *Indian art (Satavahana period):*
Marble reliefs from the Stupa of Amaravati
(1st–2nd century AD). British Museum,
London.

18   *Indian art (Satavahana period) : Carved panel showing the Stupa of Amaravati. British Museum, London.*

19   *Indian art (Satavahana period) : Reliefs from the*
Stupa of Amaravati (1st–2nd century AD). (Above)
National Museum, Madras. (Below) British Museum,
London.

from the ancient Buddhist reliquaries of Bimaran and Kanishka, which were undoubtedly indebted to Hellenistic jewellers, and ivories from Begram in Afghanistan which, by contrast, are typical expressions of Satavahana art. They can also be compared with the costly objects which have been excavated at Taxila, a city which was conquered by Alexander the Great, the Mauryans and the Scythians. Hardly any of the buildings of Taxila have survived, but the terracotta objects, the small statues and the jewellery which have been uncovered in the soil of this ancient city prove that it was a meeting-point of many cultures and traditions.

During the Kushan dynasty the region of Gandhara, which corresponds to the wide Kabul Valley, was active and flourishing. In the first centuries of the Christian era it developed a school of art which is sometimes called Graeco-Buddhist but also has much in common with provincial Roman art of the Middle East. Its architecture and sacred sculpture were largely inspired by Buddhism, the official religion of the Kushan dynasty. The stupas of Gandhara are more advanced than Mauryan and Sunga types, with a tendency towards a more elegant and vertical shape. A cylindrical drum now appears between the platform and the hemisphere, joining the hemisphere to form a kind of tower crowned by a series of umbrellas. The reliefs and statues on the sacred buildings are much more mature than before, both stylistically and in their religious expression. In the Gandharan civilization Buddha is no longer seen as

20 *Indian art (school of Gandhara) : Fragment of a seal from Taxila. National Museum, Karachi.*

21 *Indian art (school of Gandhara) : Head of Bodhisattva
from Taxila (5th century AD). National Museum,
Karachi.*

20   Indian art (school of Gandhara): *Fragment of a seal from Taxila*. National Museum, Karachi.
This fragment of a seal is something of a rarity because of its round rather than rectangular shape and because it features human figures.

21   Indian art (school of Gandhara): *Head of Bodhisattva from Taxila* (5th century AD). National Museum, Karachi.
The Gandharan civilization adapted many elements of Hellenistic art to the interpretation of its own Indian themes.

22   Indian art (Satavahana period): *Two young girls, ivory panel from Begram*. Musée Guimet, Paris.
This is one of a series of small tablets that charmingly illustrate scenes in the daily life of a harem.

23   Indian art (Kushan period): *Small stupa from the Swat Valley*. Museum of Indian Art, Calcutta.
The small Stupa of Swat stands on a square, decorated base; after the three tiers supporting the cupola seven crowning umbrellas considerably increase the overall height of the stupa, but make for an effect that is oddly out of balance with the base.

24   Indian art (school of Gandhara): *Scene from the life of Buddha* (2nd century AD). Freer Gallery of Art, Washington, DC.
The most important innovation the artists of Gandhara brought to Indian art was the representation of Buddha as a person. The robed body is portrayed with great simplicity – in marked contrast to the more active, gesticulating attendant figures.

25   Indian art (school of Mathura): *Group of bacchante, relief from Mathura* (2nd century AD). National Museum, New Delhi.
Sensual gaiety radiates from these voluptuous high-relief female figures.

22   *Indian art (Satavahana period) : Two young girls, ivory panel from Begram. Musée Guimet, Paris.*

23 Indian art (Kushan period): Small stupa from the Swat Valley. Museum of Indian Art, Calcutta

24   *Indian art (school of Gandhara) : Scene from the life of Buddha
(2nd century AD). Freer Gallery of Art, Washington, DC.*

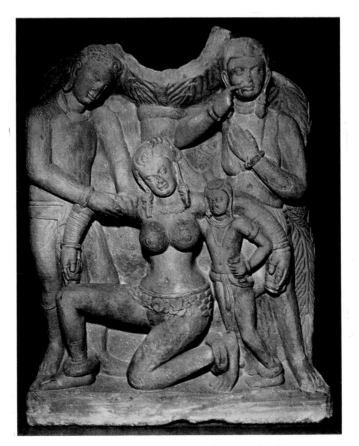

25   *Indian art (school of Mathura) : Group of bacchante,
relief from Mathura (2nd century AD). National Museum,
New Delhi.*

a supernatural, inaccessible being who manifests himself in nirvana or in mystical ecstasies. Instead, he is seen as a practical example of charity and piety, like the figure of Bodhisattva, who, while following in Buddha's footsteps, renounced nirvana to live among men in a spirit of love. Naturally the sculpture is influenced by these ideas and gives the pious Buddha a human face, a face reminiscent of elegant Graeco-Roman models. The subjects the artists seem to prefer for their reliefs in schist (a very plentiful material in this area) and their round stucco reliefs are scenes connected with Buddha: episodes in his life, his miraculous appearances and his death. The compositions are well balanced and clearly derived from the west, and the crowds of people and minor deities that surround Buddha seem like Buddhist versions of Greek or Roman gods. The aesthetic quality of these works is uneven. Sometimes they come close to being masterpieces, but often they are rather mediocre, and the observer is constantly made aware of the difficulty of reconciling western realism with the innate mysticism of the Indian temperament.

The Gandharan style developed gradually, learning first from the art of Mathura and later from that of Gupta; but as it became more refined and abstract, it slowly declined. Towards the fourth century the style of Hadda (a small town near Kabul) evolved within the Gandharan school. It was characterized by its stylistic maturity, a tenderness in the handling of physical features and by a perfection of form

26   *Indian art (school of Gandhara) : Female figure
from Taxila (5th century AD). National Museum,
Karachi.*

27 Indian art
(school of
Gandhara) : Head
of Bodhisattva in
stucco from Hadda,
Afghanistan (3rd–
4th century AD).
Musée Guimet,
Paris.

28 Indian art :
Stone head with
ram's horns from
Bhutesvar Tila
(c. 1st century
AD). Curzon
Museum,
Mathura.

26   Indian art (school of Gandhara): *Female figure from Taxila* (5th century AD). National Museum, Karachi.
The most famous centre of Gandharan art was Taxila in the upper region of the Indus. Important archaeological finds, including many sculptures, have been made there.

27   Indian art (school of Gandhara): *Head of Bodhisattva* in stucco from Hadda, Afghanistan (3rd–4th century AD). Musée Guimet, Paris.
The hair falls in soft waves to the neck, blending with a profile of great purity that suggests inner harmony and understanding.

28   Indian art: *Stone head with ram's horns* from Bhutesvar Tila (*c.* 1st century AD). Curzon Museum, Mathura.
Two ram's horns, the symbol of legal power, enclose a head marked by stern and forbidding features.

29   Indian art (school of Mathura): *Figure of a dancing yakshi*, relief in reddish sandstone (2nd century AD). Victoria and Albert Museum, London.
The voluptuous yakshi of Mathura art served to promote the joys of fecundity and sex and was featured often on the outer enclosures of Buddhist temples, where, as a representative of the transitory pleasures, she made a pointed contrast to the inner peace encountered in the presence of Buddha.

30, 31   Indian art (Gupta period): *Terracotta figures of Buddha (left) and Bodhisattva Padmapani (right)* from Mirpur Khas, Sind (end of 4th century AD). Prince of Wales Museum, Bombay.
In Gupta works Buddhist spirituality is expressed through linear purity in clear, harmonious forms that are idealistic but also full of life.

29 *Indian art (school of Mathura) : Figure of a dancing
yakshi, relief in reddish sandstone (2nd century AD).
Victoria and Albert Museum, London.*

30　*Indian art (Gupta period) : Terracotta figure of Buddha from Mirpur Khas, Sind (end of 4th century AD). Prince of Wales Museum, Bombay.*

31   *Indian art (Gupta period) : Terracotta figure
of Bodhisattva Padmapani from Mirpur Khas, Sind
(end of 4th century AD). Prince of Wales Museum,
Bombay.*

that links the stucco Buddhas of Hadda with the Apollos of the late Hellenistic period. The western culture that shaped the civilization of Gandhara and the neighbouring regions did not extend to the interior of India, which remained untouched by Hellenism. Thus two very different worlds existed side by side, the one ripened by contact with a foreign civilization, the other traditional, independent, unformed and in search of a unifying element.

The meeting-point of these two worlds was the city of Mathura, an important and flourishing cultural and commercial centre situated at the junction of many routes in a fertile, pleasant area. Destroyed and rebuilt many times, occupied by the Parthians and at one time serving as the summer residence of the Kushans, Mathura was an open door between east and west. The art of the region reflects the increasing impact of Indian tradition on the imported culture. The architecture and sculpture of Mathura are at first sight similar to that of Gandhara, but the spirit has changed. The Graeco-Roman forms have only been borrowed because they can be used to express typically Indian ideals and ideas. The reliefs and statues of Buddha, Bodhisattva, the nymphs and minor gods have a composure and serenity which, at its best, owes nothing to Gandhara or Hellenism. In particular, the sculptures of Mathura provide a profound and solemn interpretation of the life of Buddha's which is in complete sympathy with the deepest Indian spiritual feelings.

When India was still a stranger to western culture,

there was a mixture of religions and beliefs, languages and dialects, philosophical ideas and literature waiting to be combined into a single tradition which would express India's own nationality. On the religious and cultural levels the union happened slowly and spontaneously, as various popular beliefs came together in Hinduism and the use of Sanscrit increased in educated circles.

In the political sphere the Gupta, a small provincial dynasty, interpreted this nationalist feeling. Starting from Bihar, the Gupta conquered northern and central India and finally joined the south to the Deccan. Their reign symbolized the ultimate glorification of the Indian spirit and is considered a golden age in Indian history which successive ages strove to copy. The old Hindu religion, which until then had been mainly followed by the masses, triumphed. It was divided into the main cults of Vishnu, Krishna and Shiva, who were surrounded by a host of minor deities, and it offered new and rich possibilities for artistic development. The cultural and philosophical heritage which had been handed down from the time of the sacred Vedas and codified and brought together became part of a new civilization that had made positive contact with the west.

Gupta society flourished. In character it was aristocratic, educated and, above all, truly Indian. It would not be accurate to say that the art of this period was entirely religious, because there was no real distinction between religious and secular activities. To the Indian, religion is the vital spark that informs every

32　*Indian art (Gupta period) : Head of Buddha, from Mathura. Curzon Museum, Mathura.*

33 *Indian art (Gupta period) : Relief of couple in terracotta, from Yamuna (5th century AD). Curzon Museum, Mathura.*

34   *Indian art : General view of the caves of Ajanta in the Deccan (2nd century BC – 6th century AD).*

35 *Indian art (Gupta period) : Detail of the façade of Chaitya No. **19** in the caves of Ajanta (first half of **6**th century AD).*

32   Indian art (Gupta period): *Head of Buddha*, from Mathura. Curzon Museum, Mathura.

This is a typical Gupta head of the Buddha, with conventionalized features, hair conveyed by a repeat pattern in the snail-shell style and the ushnisha or cranial protuberance rising out of the top of the skull.

33   Indian art (Gupta period): *Relief of couple in terracotta*, from Yamuna (5th century AD). Curzon Museum, Mathura.

This scene, possibly representing a harem, is invested with a harsh realism, exaggerated to the point of grotesqueness.

34   Indian art: *General view of the caves of Ajanta in the Deccan* (2nd century BC – 6th century AD).

In 1819 a group of soldiers discovered by chance a series of twenty-nine Buddhist sanctuaries near the source of the Waghora river. These had been hollowed out from the rocks over a period of several centuries.

35, 36   Indian art (Gupta period): *Details of the façade of Chaitya No. 19 in the caves of Ajanta* (first half of 6th century AD).

The cave-temples are of two different kinds: the *viharas*, or caves for living in, and the *chaityas*, or meeting places that were used for prayer. Chaitya No. 19 belongs to the most splendid period of Ajanta: two massive columns decorated with floral friezes support the porch, above which is a horseshoe-shaped window. The sides, pillars and walls are decorated with figures of Buddha.

37   Indian art (Gupta period): *Interior of Chaitya No. 26 in the caves of Ajanta* (first half of 6th century AD).

Chaitya No. 26, built some years after No. 19, is more richly and elaborately ornamented. The great hall, about seventy-five feet long and forty feet wide, has twenty-six columns and an elegant stupa with a carved figure of Buddha. Above is an ornate frieze.

36   *Indian art (Gupta period) : Part of the façade of Chaitya No. 19 in the caves of Ajanta (first half of 6th century AD).*

37   *Indian art (Gupta period) : Interior of Chaitya No. 26 in the caves of Ajanta (first half of 6th century AD).*

deed and thought, and the common denominator of the many beliefs is the co-existence of mysticism and a joyous sensuality. It is important to grasp these ideas if we are to understand Gupta and Medieval Hindu art, which continued to develop these two sides of human aspiration in an art rich in subject matter, warm and alive but never realistic because it always kept to set rules and formal symbols.

The Gupta emperors were devoted to the god Vishnu and built many temples in his honour, but only a few, such as those at Citorgarh and Gwalior, have survived. They are the prototypes of the typical Hindu temple, which was later elaborated and enriched but never substantially changed. It originally consisted of a single square cella (*garbha griha*) with a portico. This was later raised on a platform and surrounded by a cloister which was reached by a flight of stairs. Much later more tiers and side chapels were added. The basic characteristics of Hindu architecture are the almost total lack of circular or spherical lines, which are replaced by emphasis on the horizontal and the vertical, and the elaboration of the columns that rose, from a square base, into many-sided and finally rounded sections. The Hindu temple, like the Buddhist stupa, was a symbol designed to represent an image of the world. Among the Buddhist buildings of the Gupta period is the Mahabodhi temple, built in the sixth century at Bodh-Gaya in honour of Buddha.

The development of sculpture already started by the school of Mathura reached its peak in the reign of the

Gupta. The sculptors were gifted artists with great technical skill, and instead of following their own impulse or trying to portray reality faithfully, they obeyed a series of prescribed rules under the guidance of the priests. Thus the Gupta sculptures which are found in large quantities in the sacred temples seem more the result of strict and accurate study than the creations of a free imagination. Bodies were often made to echo the movements and attitudes of dancing, which was considered one of the most important art forms. The portrayal of female beauty was of special importance and works had to be seductive and to suggest love and joy. The gods are shown with the symbols of their power, and Vishnu often appears on an eagle with his consort Laksmi. The rhythm and harmony of dancing dominate every relief composition and give a sacred, almost ritual aura even to evidently profane scenes.

In the Deccan, Gupta art is found mainly in the monasteries built in caves, which are richly decorated with frescoes and sculptures. These caves, which are partly Hindu, are particularly important because they contain almost the only examples of paintings of the Gupta period which have survived. Outstanding among these are the famous caves of Ajanta, which were constructed at various periods from the beginning of the second century BC and were decorated with a vast series of frescoes, notably in the fifth and sixth centuries. Although the major part have been severely damaged, they show that Gupta painting was not inferior to its architecture and sculpture.

Portraits of court life, love scenes, feasts and processions take their place with the figures of deities and sacred episodes on the walls of the caves. The outlines are faintly indicated, with an exquisite sense of rhythm and ornamentation, and the colours are applied in solid blocks with delicate shading. After the sixth century outlines became more accentuated and figures more opulent and majestic. Decadence was approaching and it resulted, politically, in the fall of the Gupta, who were overwhelmed by the White Huns and replaced, until the eighth century, by various minor kings who were often hostile to each other and tried in vain to continue the Gupta tradition. All the arts declined and gradually a cold, empty imitation replaced the inspired art that formerly had reflected an ideal community. At many of the provincial courts the tradition of a glorious past petered out in trivial shows of luxury and pomp.

In the fifth century, when the expansion of the Gupta kingdom reached the Deccan, bringing with it among other things its own Hindu cults, many colonies of faithful Jainists took refuge in the south, where several dynasties who later took a leading role in Indian civilization and art were to make their appearance. This is one reason why the art of northern and central India, and in particular of the Gupta, was introduced into the south, where it mixed with local elements. At Aihole, a small town south of Bombay, there are traces of the first capital of the Chalukyas, a dynasty that reigned over part of southern India with changing fortune until the eighth

38   *Indian art (post-Gupta dynasty) : Hindu temple at Citorgarh.*

39   *Indian art (Gupta period) : Temple of Mahabodhi*
at Bodh-Gaya (AD 526).

40 *Indian art : Apsara from a fresco
outside Vihara No. 17 in the caves of Ajanta
(5th century AD).*

41   *Indian art : Palace scene, from a fresco in Vihara No. 1 in the caves of
Ajanta (middle of 6th century AD).*

43   *Indian art : Scene from the Visvantara jataka, a fresco in Vihara No. 17 in the caves of Ajanta (5th century AD).*

century. The temples of Aihole, together with the later ones at Vatapi (now Badami) and Pattadakal, show the gradual development of Chalukya architecture. The first buildings seem very simple, but they have a fascination that stems from their sober composition. In the temples of the seventh century the Gupta style is triumphant, and the buildings are more complicated and adorned with numerous sculptures. In the final stage the Gupta influence was slowly replaced by new ideas derived from the architecture of the neighbouring kingdom of Pallava. The taste for grandeur, which was typical of the final stage of Chalukya art, can be seen on a vast scale in the temples hollowed out in the rocks at Ellora and Elephanta.

While the twelfth- and thirteenth-century Pandyas, who succeeded the Chola in south India, left various traces of their artistic activity, hardly anything survives from their first reign, which was contemporary with those of the Chalukya and the Pallava. The first southern dynasty to produce their own civilization, with an art totally independent from the north, was the Pallava. They were first and foremost creators, while the part played by the Chalukyas was not so much creative as interpretative. During this period (the seventh century) the most widespread cults in the south were those of Shiva and Vishnu, which were followed by the majority of the people and their chosen rulers. It was these cults that inspired the religious architecture of the Pallavas, of which the most famous and sumptuous examples are at Mamalla-

44   *Indian art (Chalukya period) : Façade of Chaitya No. 10
in the caves of Ellora (6th–9th century AD).*

45   *Indian art (Chalukya period) : Reliefs from Sanctuary
No. 21 in the caves of Ellora (6th–9th century AD).*

44, 45 Indian art (Chalukya period): Façade of *Chaitya* No. 10 (*above*) and reliefs from Sanctuary No. 21 (*below*) from the caves of Ellora (6th–9th centuries AD).

The façade of this Buddhist *chaitya*, complete with loggia and balcony, presents an imposing spectacle to the approaching worshipper. The sanctuary (lower picture) is one of the most interesting Hindu caves. It is vigorously decorated with high reliefs, with the figure of Shiva prominent.

46 Indian art (Pallava period): *Monolithic Temple of Bhima* at Mamallapuram (7th century AD).

Among the most typical creations of this period are the monolithic temples of Mamallapuram, each one carved from a single block of rock.

47 Indian art (Pallava period): *The Shore Temple* at Mamallapuram (8th century AD).

This many-tiered, pyramidal temple is built conven-

46   *Indian art (Pallava period) : Monolithic Temple of Bhima at Mamallapuram (7th century AD).*

tionally of stone blocks, unlike the monolith shown opposite.

48   Indian art (Chalukya period): *Vishnu sleeping on a coiled serpent*, a relief in Sanctuary No. 9 at Aihole (6th century AD). Prince of Wales Museum, Bombay.
Vishnu lies on the coiled body of the World Serpent, its seven heads forming a halo around his head.

49   Indian art (Chalukya period): *Hermaphrodite Shiva*, a relief in the cave of Elephanta near Bombay (8th century AD).
The god here presents masculine and feminine aspects that refer to his dual nature as creator and destroyer.

50   Indian art (Pallava period): *Hindu temple* at Nattalamai (8th century AD).
The principal structure of this Hindu temple represents Mount Meru, the seat of the gods, and is crowned with a cupola symbolizing the vault of the heavens.

47   *Indian art (Pallava period) : The Shore Temple at Mamallapuram (8th century AD).*

48 Indian art (Chalukya period) : Vishnu sleeping on a coiled serpent, a relief in Sanctuary No. 9 at Aihole (6th century AD). Prince of Wales Museum, Bombay.

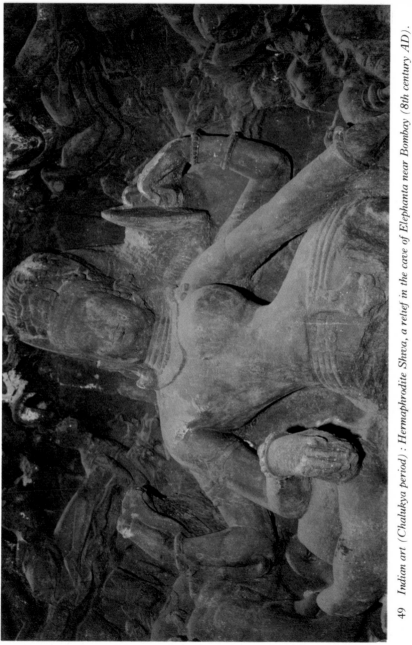

49 Indian art (Chalukya period): Hermaphrodite Shiva, a relief in the cave of Elephanta near Bombay (8th century AD).

puram. There is a group of many-tiered temples, mainly pyramid-shaped, elaborately designed and decorated externally in a baroque style. The sculptures resemble those of the Gupta in their elegant proportions and expressive intensity, but they are more monumental and come closer to the concept of the god. They are solemn works of art, the fruit of sincere inspiration, and are the final masterpieces of the classical period of Indian art.

At the end of the Gupta period the territory of northern and central India was divided into various military states which were often at war with each other. The character of the new society that developed with the rise of these states was reflected in their cultural and artistic activity. The court and nobles of the new states formed a privileged elite who encouraged the gods to be favourable by making generous gifts to the priests of the temples. Ordinary people were excluded from the official ceremonies of the cult, which were presided over by the ruling families, and in the hands of corrupt priests and upper-class laymen it degenerated into idolatry. The idol venerated in the temple was treated as a real person, and a complicated ceremonial governed the meals, rest, amusements and wishes of the god. This explains the grandeur and luxury of many of the temples, which were built by the rulers to assert their own power. The dazzling richness of certain external details and the profane and often erotic character of the sculptures that adorn the temples reflect the nature of the ceremonies that took place there.

70 *Indian art (Pallava period) : Hindu temple at Nattalamai (8th century AD).*

At the same time, in the extreme north, the regions of Bengal and Kashmir became the seats of powerful rulers. The first, after being plundered by barbarians who invaded the frontier, enjoyed a fortunate period under the Pala dynasty, which succeeded the Sena in the twelfth century. In olden times the Bengalese people had worshipped some unsavoury gods including the black goddess Kali, but gradually they accepted Buddhism and added to it many local variations including the worship of female deities. Pala and Sena art refers to these cults and many stupas were built, some in the form of towers and some on the model of Hindu temples. The sculpture that appeared about the eighth century was still rather fanciful, but the modelling was lively and incisive. In the tenth century a notable development produced graceful, elegant figures full of inner life but later, with the arrival of the Sena, the elegance was transformed into uninspired coldness. There was also a separate group in Pala and Sena art that made bronzes. These usually depict idols and are nearly always exquisitely made. The few miniatures of the Pala period that have survived show a similar development to that of Gupta painting. Beginning with simple but effective forms and lines, they progressed to more elaborate styles that were cold and superficial.

In Kashmir a succession of dynasties waged unceasing war with their neighbours and the region was artistically less fortunate than Bengal until it was occupied by the Moslems. But under the Karkota and later the Utpala it enjoyed a flourishing period that coincided

51 *Indian art (Sena period) : Mother and child, a stele from Gangarampur (12th century AD). Museum of Indian Art, Calcutta.*

52 *Indian art (Medieval period) : Stele bearing the figure of Trivikrama, from Dinajpur (10th century AD). Museum of Indian Art Calcutta.*

53 *Indian art (Pala or Sena period): Stele showing the figure of Vishnu, from Bengal (11th–12th century). Metropolitan Museum of Art, New York.*

51   Indian art (Sena period): *Mother and child*, a stele from Gangarampur (12th century). Museum of Indian Art, Calcutta.

One characteristic of Sena sculpture is an exaggerated striving for decorative effect which betrays itself in the slightly forced pose of the figures and the superficial treatment of the face; ornaments, on the other hand, appear fussy and overworked.

52   Indian art (Medieval period): *Stele bearing the figure of Trivikrama*, from Dinajpur (10th century). Museum of Indian Art, Calcutta.

In spite of the continual struggle between the various local dynasties, Indian art did not cease to flourish in the medieval period although artists were obliged to remain within the bounds of local characteristics.

53   Indian art (Pala or Sena period): *Stele showing the figure of Vishnu*, from Bengal (11th–12th centuries). Metropolitan Museum of Art, New York.

This is a complicated structure weighty with ornamental motifs; the concept is grandiose but the work is artificial and comparatively minor.

54   Indian art (Pratihara period): (*Left*) *Tara* (9th century). National Museum, New Delhi. (*Right*) *Ashtabhuja Marichi* (9th century). Museum of Indian Art, Calcutta.

Officially followers of the Hindu religion, the Pratiharas were strongly attracted to magic, which led them to create numerous religious buildings and divine images.

55   Indian art (Medieval period): *Interior of Jain temple* at Dilvara, Mount Abu (11th century).

The Jain temples, built entirely in white marble, have fantastic sculptural decorations which combine the pomp and richness of a fairy-tale palace with an extraordinary delicacy and lightness.

54   *Indian art (Pratihara period) : (Left) Tara (9th century AD).
National Museum, New Delhi. (Right) Ashtabhuja Marichi (9th century AD).
Museum of Indian Art, Calcutta.*

with a notable artistic development. Both architecturally and sculpturally the art of Kashmir illustrates the meeting-point of Roman and Gupta Indian motifs. The real founders of the architecture typical of the Medieval Hindu period were the Pratihara princes, the rulers of the Gujerat tribe whose ancient capital was Kanauj. These princes, who governed a kingdom in the heart of India which branched out to north and south, did not keep their power for long but split up into a number of minor kingdoms such as those of the Chandellas, the Cahamanas, the Paramaras, etc., and each used and encouraged the leading Pratihara artists.

Superstitious and fanatical worshippers of various Hindu deities, the Pratiharas dedicated huge, cathedral-like temples to their idols. The most typical structure was one in which the temple was raised on a platform and consisted of an open anteroom, a closed cult room, a portico and a sanctuary surrounded by terraces. In another part of the temple was a communal dining-room and baths and additional chapels. The unexpected contrast between the dark entrance and the light from the golden lamps which surrounded the idol in the sanctuary must have been very impressive. There are splendid Hindu temples at Khajuraho, the capital of the Chandellas, at Konarak in Orissa, at Udaypur in the Malva region and many other places. They are never mere repetitions but always new versions of the same rules. There are extra buildings based on a variety of formulas and structures which become more compli-

55   *Indian art (Medieval period) : Interior of Jain temple at Dilvara, Mount Abu (11th century).*

cated and daring in their design. Indian architecture of the medieval period reveals an inexhaustible understanding of form which is constantly resolved in exuberant and fantastic ways.

As well as the temples dedicated to Hindu idols, particularly in Orissa the followers of the Jain cult built sacred buildings characterized by the plentiful use of white marble. Most famous are the Mount Abu temples at Dilvara and Alchargah. Other contemporary Jain buildings, like those at Citorgarh, are similar. The Jain temple had its own sanctuary enclosed in a kind of courtyard, off which opened

56 *Indian art (Rashtrakuta period) : Kailasa temple at Ellora (8th century).*

twenty-four chapels dedicated to the Tirthankara. The first Pratihara temples were like this, but their descendants covered them with sculptures of the deity and numerous seductive female images and erotic scenes. These can be seen in the decoration of the temples of Orissa and Malva, which are particularly flamboyant. The aesthetic quality of the sculptures is uneven, because sometimes they are the work of great artists and sometimes, evidently, of simple apprentices and workmen. There are many dazzling and inventive compositions, articulated by a sublime rhythm which makes the subject seem to

57   *Indian art
(Chola period) :
The central
sanctuary of the
Brihadisvara
Temple at Tanjore
(c. 1000–12).*

56   Indian art (Rashtrakuta period): *Kailasa Temple* at Ellora (8th century).
The Indian technique of 'excavated' architecture reached its peak in the Kailasa of Ellora. Two hundred thousand tons of rock were removed to isolate the monolith in which the temple is hollowed out.

57   Indian art (Chola dynasty): *The central sanctuary of the Brihadisvara Temple* at Tanjore (*c.* 1000–12).
Among the various temples built by the Cholas, the grandest was the one at Tanjore erected by the emperor Rajaraja the Great. The summit of the central sanctuary (*vimana*) was about 235 feet high and is decorated with many architectural and sculptural motifs. The *vimana* was crowned by a gigantic monolithic cupola weighing about eighty tons. According to tradition it was raised to this height along an incline that stretched nearly four miles from the temple.

58   Indian art (Pandya period): *North portal of the Temple of Shiva Nataraja* at Chidambaram (12th century).
In temples in the Dravidian or Southern style the importance of the chief sanctuary (*vimana*) is often over-shadowed by the great portals (*gopuras*) that reach extraordinary dimensions. They are multi-tiered like the *vimana* and culminate in a barrel-vault enclosed by great fan-shaped arches.

59   Indian art (Medieval period): *Wheel of the sun-chariot*, a detail from the Surya Temple at Konarak (middle of 12th century).
The Surya temple at Konarak is one of the greatest achievements of Indian architecture. Its structure re-produces the celestial chariot of Surya (the sun god) the wheels resting on the base. The dimensions are enormous, and the fine detail of the sculptural decoration represents a masterpiece of carving.

58   *Indian art (Pandya period) : North portal of the Temple of Shiva Nataraja at Chidambaram (12th century).*

move. But there are also many crude figures which lack inspiration or feeling.

Completely independent from the Pratihara was the Rashtrakuta dynasty which reigned in the Deccan, dividing the territory with the Chalukya in the west. The art of the Rashtrakuta rulers shows a clear difference between north and south. The temples are developed in a horizontal rather than a vertical sense, and the relationship between the various parts is not smooth and gradual but harsh and abrupt. Like the sculptures of the south, the architecture is given to violent contrasts, strong light and shade and broken lines. The decoration of these temples has a richness, variety and joyousness that takes the breath away. The statues have the vitality and immediacy of the sacred southern dances. Only later, with the Kakatiya and Yodava dynasties, does the sculpture become more restrained and stylized.

Still further south is the region of the Cholas (*c* 985– 13th century), the dynasty which had the distinction of bringing unity and peace to southern India. Architecturally the Cholas were the heirs of the Chalukyas and the Pallavas. Their temples consisted of a one-storey room for worship and a sanctuary with three storeys. Later on, a vast cupola and majestic portals (*gopuras*) were added. The Cholas built temples in about seventy southern cities, and some of the most beautiful examples are those at Srirangam and Trivandrum. The temples of the Pandya dynasty, which succeeded the Cholas for a short time, are smaller and more elegant. The

59   *Indian art (Medieval period) : Wheel of the sun-chariot, a detail from the Surya Temple at Konarak, (middle of 12th century).*

sculpture of the Cholas represents not so much the creation of a new age as the continuation, at a distance, of the preceding civilization. It lacks the resources of energy and vitality that usually accompany a new artistic style, but it has the grace and refinement of a declining culture. Later a popular reaction resulted in more lively and immediate sculpture. Particularly beautiful are the Chola bronzes which include the well-known model of Shiva dancing in a circle of flames.

Already in the eighth century the Moslems, thirsty to extend their territory, had threatened the borders of India from time to time. In the tenth century a Turkish-Moslem kingdom was set up at Ghazna in Afghanistan, so close to India to be a constant danger to the northern states. But it was not until 1196 that the resistance of the Hindu states was finally overcome by the Sultan Aibek, who entered Delhi, which later became the capital of his new sultanate. Soon the Moslems had dominated a large part of southern and central India including the Deccan, and Moslem art forced its way into the heart of ancient India, mixing with local secular traditions, introducing new idols, and initially creating a conflict of taste and style— though this eventually produced a positive result.

By the twelfth century Hindu art was becoming exhausted and its examples now seem cold and conventional. Moslem art, born in a very different spiritual climate and physical surroundings, showed India new roads, substituting for fantastic and irrational architecture a mathematical sense of propor-

60 *Indian art (Chola dynasty) : Shiva Nataraja, processional bronze (12th century). National Museum, New Delhi.*

61   *Indian art (Moslem period) : The Qutb al-Minar,*
Delhi (end of 12th century – beginning of 16th century).

62   *Indian art (Moslem period) : Remains of the Quwwat al-Islam
Mosque, Delhi (1193).*

63   *Indian art (Moslem period) : The Great Mosque at Ajmer (beginning of 13th century).*

64   *Indian art (Moslem period) : Mausoleum of 'Isa Khan,*
Delhi (1547).

60   Indian art (Chola dynasty): Shiva Nataraja, proces-
sional bronze (12th century). National Museum, New
Delhi.
Dancing is an outward expression of the power of Shiva.
At his pleasure he can create and destroy.

61, 62   Indian art (Moslem period): *The Qutb al-Minar*
(end of 12th century – beginning of 16th century) and the
remains of the *Quwwat al-Islam Mosque*, Delhi (1193).
The minaret was used as an observatory as well as a
monument celebrating Aibek's victory in north India.
At its feet are the ruins of the first Indian mosque, the
Quwwat al-Islam.

63   Indian art (Moslem period): *The Great Mosque* at
Ajmer (beginning of 13th century).
Only fragments of the Great Mosque have survived. Some
of the most important remains are these columns, with
their graceful shafts enriched with horizontal bands of
restrained and elegant calligraphic decoration.

64   Indian art (Moslem period): *Mausoleum of Isa Khan*,
Delhi (1547).
The mausoleum of Isa Khan is a fine example of the
harmony and elegance which are so characteristic of the
Islamic style.

65   Indian art (Hindu revival period): *The toilet of Radha
Rajput Pahari* (18th–19th centuries). Freer Gallery of Art,
Washington, DC.
The graceful female figure, displayed in a seductive yet
remote pose, gives this miniature a special charm.

66   Indian art (Moslem period): *Young man intent on
reading* (beginning of 17th century). Freer Gallery of
Art, Washington, DC.
In the peaceful setting of a pleasant garden a youth, one
slipper on the ground, is absorbed in his reading.

65   *Indian art (Hindu revival period) : The toilet of Radha
Rajput Pahari (18th–19th century). Freer Gallery of Art,
Washington, DC.*

66   *Indian art (Moslem period) : Young man
intent on reading (beginning of 17th century).
Freer Gallery of Art, Washington, DC.*

tion and construction, for figurative and naturalistic sculpture a geometrical and abstracted ornamental elegance, and for watery and toned-down colours a new vividness and extraordinary luminosity. In the first ten years of the thirteenth century, the first mosque was built on Indian soil at Quwwat al-Islam, and there rose in Delhi the Qutb al-Minar, the great red minaret that celebrated the Moslem victory. The first Moslem mosques were built by using the remains of old Hindu buildings, but in the Qutb al-Minar, as in the Arhai-din-ka-jhonpra at Ajmer, we find the pure Moslem style. This is to be seen in the fringed pointed arch, the columns formed by groups of pillars, and the harmonious cupolas covering the vast areas where the faithful met.

The Moslem reign did not last long in India as a political unit. Between 1348–1412 internal rebellions and threats of invasion from outside resulted in a series of regional sultanates which were often at war with each other. In each region a Moslem style developed with minor variations dependent on surviving local traditions. Among the most beautiful buildings were those built in the neighbourhood of Delhi and at Hairpur by the Lodi sultans. The Lodi mosque at Hairpur and the later mausoleums of Ser Sah and 'Isa Khan are masterpieces of elegance and harmony carried out in the classic Islamic style. In Delhi and Malva the architecture faithfully follows Islamic models, but in other regions such as Kashmir, Bengal and Gujarat it is linked to the Hindu tradition and the mosques seem like adaptations of the Hindu temple and are sometimes built of the same materials (brick in Bengal and sandstone in Gujarat).

In the Deccan, where the resistance of the southern regions resulted in an almost continuous state of war, the sultans had to employ gangs of mercenaries from Persia. Thus the architecture here shows signs of Persian influence, with square towers, terraces and tall arched doors. Only later, when the Moslems occupied the kingdoms of Vijayangar, was the Persian influence joined to that of southern Hinduism. An art which developed particularly from the fourteenth century onwards was miniature painting, which was used to decorate sacred and profane manuscripts. The earliest examples are in a composite

67 *Indian art (Hindu revival period) : General view of the monuments of Ranakpur and the Jain temple of Mount Abu (15th century).*

style which is chiefly Persian but has some Hindu characteristics, especially in the details. Vivid colours are used and the scenes are planned as harmonious and rhythmic compositions. The design itself is flat; the liveliness in these works springs from the action. The most beautiful miniatures are those in the Rajput style of the princes of Rajasthan, who rebelled against the Moslems at the end of the fourteenth century. Their uprising is linked to a kind of Hindu revival which was artistic and spiritual although it was concerned mainly with religious reform. The fanatical worship of idols and the superstition of the end of the medieval period were replaced by faith in a single, kind, protective god, who stood above all else for love.

67   Indian art (Hindu revival period): *General view of the monuments of Ranakpur and the Jain temple of Mount Abu* (15th century).
Art took a nationalist stand at this period. It reacted against the Moslem style and revived the forms and outlines of the Indian traditions of the medieval period.

68   Indian art (Hindu revival period): *Cloister of the Ramesvaram Temple* (12th century).
The cloisters of the Ramesvaram Temple are about two and a half miles long. This impressive row is adorned with highly elaborate motifs.

69   Indian art (Hindu revival period): *Pillars of the mandapa of the Srirangam Temple* (15th century). The *mandapas* were 'porch-type' shrines, where the pilgrims rested after their journey and dances and ceremonies were held.

68

70 Indian art (Hindu revival period): *Gopuras or portals of the Srirangam Temple* (15th century).
Like all Dravidian temples of the period, the Srirangam Temple is enormous. The vast circle of its walls could almost enclose a whole city.

71 Indian art (Moghul period): *The Taj Mahal,* Agra (1630–48).
The building has an octagonal plan and is crowned with a vast cupola and surrounded by four minarets. The façade is varied and lightened by skilfully placed niches.

72 Indian art (Moghul period): *The Old Palace* of Amber (17th century).
Amber was founded in the 10th century and until 1728 it was the capital of the state of Jaipur. Good relations existed between the court of Amber and the Moghuls, and the Residency at Amber was chiefly inspired by Moghul palaces of the period.

69   *Indian art (Hindu revival period) : Pillars of the mandapa of the Srirangam Temple (15th century).*

70 *Indian art (Hindu revival period) : Gopuras or portals of the Srirangam Temple (15th century).*

71 *Indian art (Moghul period) : The Taj Mahal, Agra (1630–48).*

72   *Indian art (Moghul period) : The Old Palace of Amber (17th century).*

The god is Vishnu, incarnate as Krishna, whose affection for his wife Radha symbolizes the love of God for the good. Thus Krishna is one of the subjects most frequently portrayed in the Rajput miniatures, which interpreted the mysteries of the faith in human terms.

The only Indian kingdom that succeeded in resisting the Moslem invasion for three generations, until the beginning of the seventeenth century, was Vijayanagar, in the south. Faithful to southern artistic traditions, the Vijayanagar became the patrons of the most glorious art India has ever known. The temples built in their capital Vijayanagar, the City of Victory, and at Tanjore, Srirangam and Kumba Konam are masterpieces of architectural fantasy and decorative flamboyance. The buildings have superbly spacious porches (*mandapas*) where the faithful can mingle freely and rest after a tiring pilgrimage. The towers (*gopuras*) are enormous, but the sanctuary itself remains of modest proportions. Majestic groups of horses flank the pillars that support the roof, and one of the most extraordinary examples of lavish decoration is the hall of a thousand pillars at Srirangam, which dates partly from the period following the Vijayanagar. The style survived the fall of the kingdom in 1565 and in later centuries produced ever grander monuments such as the huge temple at Madura and the smaller, more elegant one at Tanjore dedicated to Sabramanya. Sculpture for a time maintained its force and lively spontaneity but then fell into decline; a gap opened and rapidly widened between the strict

73   *Indian art (Moghul period) : The Diwan-i hass, or pavilion for private audiences at the Red Fort, Delhi (17th century).*

116

73   Indian art (Moghul period): The *diwan-i hass*, or pavilion for private audiences.at the Red Fort, Delhi (17th century).

The Red Fort (so-called because of the red sandstone of some of the buildings) is an ornate collection of buildings founded by Shah Jehan. As well as a small mosque (to be seen in the bottom left of the photograph) the complex includes music rooms, baths and places for public and private audiences. The various parts are connected by pleasant gardens.

74   Indian art (Moghul period): *The Adoration of Krishna in the Golden City* (*c*. 1600). Freer Gallery of Art, Washington, DC.

In this elegant miniature a variety of figures move through an intricate scene of palaces and gardens. They are drawn with great skill and enriched with bright colours.

75   Indian art (Moghul period): *Mardkank Khatni brings the ring to Maltas, the prison warder* (late 16th century). Freer Gallery of Art, Washington, DC.

The miniaturists of the Moghul period particularly liked illustrating events at court, battle scenes full of movement and legends. Figures are generally arranged in groups and articulated in occasionally complicated ways; there is a strong tendency among the artists to treat faces as individual portraits.

74   *Indian art (Moghul period) : The adoration of Krishna in the Golden city (c. 1600). Freer Gallery of Art, Washington, DC.*

75   *Indian art (Moghul period): Mardkank Khatni brings the ring to Maltas, the prison warder (late 16th century). Freer Gallery of Art, Washington, DC.*

121

rules of religious ceremony and the feelings and ambitions of the artists themselves.

Profiting from the uncertain and chaotic political situation, the Moghuls from the Middle East kingdoms of Samarkand and Kabul took over India in the sixteenth century. The conquest was begun by Babur and his son Humayan, but it was the great Akbar who finally established the Moghul empire on Indian soil. He showed great foresight in choosing both Moslems and Indians as his ministers, filling his harem with native princesses and allowing the widest religious freedom. The result was a civilization and art that united the characteristics of three different races, gradually combining them to form a balanced and coherent whole. The Moghuls themselves introduced a taste for vast flower gardens with pleasing fountains and pools and octagonal ornamented buildings with broad, open rooms.

Their first capital, Delhi, was adorned with many buildings in the Moghul period. Other important cities in the kingdom were Agra, Ajmer and Fathpur, and there are many examples of the Rajput style (which corresponds to a simplified Hindu style) in the fort of Agra and the imperial palaces of Fathpur. The Indo-Islamic style is at its best in the Saih Mu'in al-din Cisti mosque at Ajmer and the Saih Salim Cisti mosque at Fathpur. An eclectic but balanced style is already evident in the imperial palace of Ajmer and the fort of Lahore, and it becomes more mature and elegant in later buildings such as the mausoleum of the emperor Jahangir, the Jahangir-

76   *Singhalese art : Heavenly nymph, fresco in the rock-cave of Sigiriya (end of 5th century AD).*

77   *Singhalese art : The Dagoba of Kiri Vehera at Polonnaruva (12th century).*

78   *Afghan art : Spirit of the Flowers, stucco figure from Hadda (5th century AD). Musée Guimet, Paris.*

79   *Singhalese art : Seated Buddha, Polonnaruva (12th century).*

76 Singhalese art: *Heavenly nymph*, from a fresco in the rock-cave of Sigiriya (end of 5th century AD).
The heavenly nymphs that adorn the rocky walls of Sigiriya have often inspired poets' imaginations. They are among the most seductive creations of painting in Ceylon.

77 Singhalese art: *The Dagoba of Kiri Vehere* at Polonnaruva (12th century).
The Dagoba of Kiri Vehere presents an outline of compelling simplicity that recaptures the restrained line and balance of buildings of an earlier period.

78 Afghan art: *Spirit of the Flowers*, stucco figure from Hadda (5th century AD). Musée Guimet, Paris.
The sculpture clearly shows the Hellenistic influence that prevailed in Afghanistan for many years.

79 Singhalese art: *Seated Buddha*. Polonnaruva (12th century). Photo by J. P. Faure.
This powerful figure is portrayed in a yoga trance, and wears the transparent mantle common among seated Buddha images of the period.

80 Nepalese art: *The figure of Bodhisattva Manjusri*, from the cover of a Pancharaksa manuscript (1150). Museum of Indian Art, Calcutta.
This figure of the Bodhisattva is drawn with elegant lines and is richly coloured.

81 Nepalese art: *Temple* at Bhaktapur (1700).
In Nepalese architecture the pagoda-type sanctuary probably derives from earlier wooden prototypes developed in India and now lost.

82 Nepalese art: *The Stupa of Sambhunathu*, near Katmandu.
This stupa, set on the hillside of Katmandu, dominates the Valley of Nepal with its spire; this terminates in a series of thirteen umbrellas representing the heavens of the gods.

80   *Nepalese art : The figure of Bodhisattva Manjusri, from the cover of a Pancharaksa manuscript (1150). Museum of Indian Art, Calcutta.*

81 *Nepalese art : Temple at Bhaktapur (1700).*

82 *Nepalese art : The Stupa of Sambhunath, near Katmandu.*

Mahal at Agra. Around 1630 the Moslem party was in the majority at court, and the consequences can be seen in the artistic field. The Taj-Mahal, the mausoleum dedicated to the wife of the Shah Jahan, belongs to this period. Following the rules of Persian Moslem architecture, the monument preserves the unreal character of a pleasant dream or of the kind of nostalgic fantasy which is closer to the Indian spirit than to the Islamic.

In the second half of the seventeenth century Moghul architecture reached its peak. The palaces were single-storey buildings and contained suites of rooms including an audience chamber and a music room and there were fabulous gardens with annexes for baths and a mosque. The whole structure seemed like a fantastic dream in which marble blended with colourful designs, arabesques, carved decorations and gay ceramics and the effect was completed by fountains and gardens full of flowers. In the following century there were already signs of the decline that continued until the destruction of the Moghul empire and the conquest of India by the British in 1818.

The Moghul emperors summoned some famous Persian artists to form a school of miniaturists at their court, which explains why the genre flourished then and how honoured it was. The Moghul miniatures are certainly the most beautiful of Indian art. A strain of lively Hindu fantasy was added to the basic characteristics of the Persian miniature and, later, a touch of naturalism derived from a knowledge of Western painting which was brought by the mission-

83 *Nepalese art : The birth of Buddha, detail from a manuscript of the Prajna paramita sutra, painted on a palm leaf (1570). Museum of Indian Art, Calcutta.*

83   Nepalese art: *The birth of Buddha*, detail from a manuscript of the *Prajna paramita sutra*, painted on a palm leaf (1570). Museum of Indian Art, Calcutta.

The tradition of illustrated manuscripts, which ceased in India with the Moslem invasion, continued to flourish in Nepal, where many late examples have come to light. The illustrations are similar to Pala paintings.

84   Tibetan art: *Banner with a scene from the life of Buddha*. Musée Guimet, Paris.

Tibetan painting is dedicated to Buddhism, which nevertheless allows it a rich choice of themes. The picture is composed according to religious rules which lay down the colours that can be used for the halo, face and body of a god.

85   Siamese art: *Bronze figure of Buddha*, from Samgaloka (15th–16th centuries). Musée Guimet, Paris.

Here the figure of Buddha is portrayed in a rigid and heavily stylized frontal pose.

86   Siamese art: *Stone head of Buddha* (7th–9th centuries). Staatliches Museum für Völkerkunde, Munich.

This stone head of Buddha is an interesting example of Siamese art before the arrival of the Thai; the modelling is sure and rhythmical and the snail-shell convention applied to the hair derives from earlier Indian work.

87   Siamese art: *Interior courtyard of the Vat Phra Keo*, Bangkok (1785).

Gigantic sentinels of fantastic and terrible appearance stand guard outside the temple of Bangkok to ward off evil spirits. Their brilliant colouring is matched in the buildings themselves, even the roofs, with their distinctive 'ox-horn' projections.

84   *Tibetan art : Banner with a scene from the life of Buddha. Musée Guimet, Paris.*

85   *Siamese art : Bronze figure of Buddha, from Samgaloka (15th–16th century). Musée Guimet, Paris.*

86   *Siamese art : Stone head of Buddha (7th–9th century). Staatliches Museum für Völkerkunde, Munich.*

aries. Flowers and birds were enchantingly portrayed from nature in a fine range of colours. About the end of the seventeenth century the principal subjects and inspiration of the miniatures were supplied by court life. The rulers and their beautiful courtesans took their place in harmonious compositions which, although perhaps lacking in intimacy, are undoubtedly the result of great skill and fine judgment. During the Moghul period the minor arts became equally refined and advanced and produced fabrics, precious brocades, ceramics and bronzes worthy of the finest Persian traditions. The decline of the Moghul empire coincided with attempts to revive the traditional Hindu style (the fantastic, baroque buildings at Tanjore in the Maharate style) and various efforts to formulate new styles have more recently been made. The British occupation brought with it European art which, in turn, offered new possibilities to Indian artists that they are still in the process of reconciling with their own natural inclinations and religious views.

CEYLON

The countries of southern Asia adjacent to India and China present an amazing richness of artistic works. There is at the same time a basic cultural unity and also a wide range of local styles. In most of the different regions artistic life flourished as a result of contact with Indian art, at first passively imitated but later the starting point for local elaborations.

87   *Siamese art : Interior courtyard of the Vat Phra Keo, Bangkok (1785).*

Ceylon, separated from the Indian continent by only a narrow strip of sea, was by its very position a natural location in which Indian civilization could expand. According to an old local tradition Buddha Sakyamuni visited it three times, and Mahinda, the son of the Mauryan king Asoka, introduced Buddhism in the third century BC. It became, with Hinduism, the chief source of artistic inspiration. The most important monuments in Ceylon are buildings of a religious nature, but there are also some outstanding secular ones. Particularly famous is the palace of King Kassapa at Sigiriya (end of the fifth century AD) which was built on top of a steep rock and can only be reached along a tunnel. A cave in the rocks of Sigiriya houses the oldest Buddhist painting in

88 *Siamese art : A Buddhist paradise, illustrated manuscript (19th century). Musée Guimet, Paris.*

Ceylon: it shows twenty-two female figures ornamented with jewels and precious clothes and dates from the end of the fifth century AD.

AFGHANISTAN

The advance of Buddhism which was halted in the south by the sea found no such obstacles inland. In the north it first reached the territory of Afghanistan and then proceeded into central Asia and the Far East. Afghanistan was a junction for the caravan routes to the east, and through it passed spices, silks and precious stones. It was a pathway between east and west, and it became the meeting-point of very different civilizations.

89   *Khmer art : Apsaras, from a relief at Angkor Vat (first half of 12th century).*

90   *Khmer art : Figure of Tara (12th–13th century). Musée Guimet, Paris.*

141

91   *Cham art: Figure of Lokesvara in the
Dong-duong style (end of 9th century).
Musée Guimet, Paris.*

92 *Cham art: Makara dragon in the Binh-dinh style (beginning of 13th century).*
Musée Guimet, Paris.

88   Siamese art: *A Buddhist paradise*, illustrated manuscript (19th century). Musée Guimet, Paris.
A group of chosen souls indulge in a series of pleasant pastimes among the flowering trees of a celestial garden.

89   Khmer art: *Apsaras*, from a relief at Angkor Vat (first half of 12th century).
Some, 1,750 apsaras or celestial dancers adorn the exterior galleries at Angkor Vat; those shown here wear the famous 'Angkor smile'.

90   Khmer art: *Figure of Tara* (12th–13th century). Musée Guimet, Paris.
This stylized image depicts Tara, a female figure who represents the transcendent wisdom to which students aspire.

91   Cham art: *Figure of Lokesvara* in the Dong-duong style (end of 9th century). Musée Guimet, Paris.
The thick lips, the large, flattened nose and the thick eyebrows are all clearly native elements.

92   Cham art: *Makara dragon* in the Binh-dinh style (beginning of 13th century). Musée Guimet, Paris.
This very ornate head clearly relates more to Chinese inspiration than to an Indian source.

93   Indonesian art: *The goddess and the monster*, detail from a Balinese sculpture in wood (*c.* 1930). Koninklijk Institut voor de Tropen, Amsterdam.
The small figure of the goddess caught in the pose of a dancing-girl is typical of the light but superbly worked carvings of Bali.

94   Laotian art: *Bronze figure of Buddha* (18th century). Musée Guimet, Paris.
Here is the traditional concept of Buddha, the Illuminated One, dressed as a monk and holding an alms bowl in his hands.

93   *Indonesian art : The goddess and the
monster, detail from a Balinese sculpture in
wood (c. **1930**). Koninklijk Institut voor de
Tropen, Amsterdam.*

145

94 *Laotian art :*
Bronze figure of
Buddha (18th
century). Musée
Guimet, Paris.

The Achaemenian empire and that of Alexander, the reign of the Kushans and the period of Sassanian domination took their turns, each leaving an indelible imprint. In consequence, Afghan art presents an extraordinary variety of artistic directions and solutions. Some aspects obviously belong to Persian art, others to Indian, and yet others to the Hellenistic world. In the most significant works, however, elements of many origins combine to create a very original art that clearly benefited from such a variety of conquests. Particularly interesting are a number of Buddhist images composed with the help of Greek solutions; the smiling Spirit of the Flowers in the Musée Guimet, Paris is one of the most important examples. The many frescoes of Buddhist themes, carried out in an impasto of straw and clay – a technique borrowed from the East—are also interesting.

NEPAL AND TIBET

A local tradition (which is not universally accepted) maintains that the historical Buddha was not born in India but at Lumbini, in Nepal. It has always been a solid stronghold of Buddhism, and at the time of the Moslem invasion thousands of the faithful found shelter there.

The oldest Nepalese examples of sculpture and architecture, which were mostly made of wood, have nearly all been destroyed. It is not therefore possible to reconstruct a complete history of Nepalese art, but it seems to have grown up as a local variation of Indian art. The surviving buildings date mainly from the fifteenth century AD and nearly all have a basic structure consisting of one large hall surmounted by one or more pyramid-shaped roofs. Inside are images of Buddhist or Hindu deities, usually made of gilt bronze encrusted with precious stones. The chief architectural monuments are in the capital, Katmandu, and include the great stupas of Sambhunath and Bodhnath, where the Nepalese representative of the Dalai Lama still lives.

Violent and fanciful, simple or intellectually refined, Tibetan art revolves around the Buddhist religion which spread into the high plains in the special form of Lamaism and soon played an important part in the spiritual and social life of the population. Cultural and artistic activities are still concentrated in the great monasteries which stand on rocky peaks dominating – physically and spiritually – the countryside. Sculpture is chiefly represented by terrible divine figures, portrayed in fierce and menacing attitudes. A multiplicity of heads and arms gives the deity the appearance of several monstrous and rapacious demons, none of them having any resemblance to human beings. The impression of flamboyant unreality is emphasized in many works by the gilding and the encrustations of turquoise, coral and lapis lazuli.

The most characteristic aspect of Tibetan painting is the religious paintings or *tanka*, which are vertical banners painted on canvas or silk and framed by heavy bands of brocade. The *tankas* are bound by a detailed series of rules that lay down, for example, the exact colours that must be used to portray each deity. The strange combinations that result often strike westerners as shrill and discordant. Also typical of Tibetan taste are ritual objects made of human bones: these are used for magical purposes, and are usually finished with beautiful metal decorations.

SIAM AND BURMA

Pointed spires and pagodas decorated with vivid ceramics, roofs curved and gilded so that they blaze under the sun's rays are features of Siamese buildings that distinguish them from those of neighbouring countries and give the surrounding countryside an undeniably fabulous atmosphere. The most remarkable feature of Siamese architecture is the result of a fairly recent conquest: the development of truly Siamese art only began in the thirteenth century AD, when the Thai (or free men) came down from southern China into the Menam Valley, where they established their permanent seat and created a new civilization, tied to that of India but original in some respects.

The splendid temples of Bangkok nearly all belong to the last two centuries. The Wat Phra Keo, which houses a small emerald statue of Buddha, was begun in 1785. A dazzling fantasy of gold, majolica and white walls makes this an unrivalled jewel.

Despite the strong influence exercised by Indian models, Burmese architecture is also very individual.

Among the green rice-fields and the tropical trees are thousands and thousands of stupas, crowned by pointed spires and spherical cupolas of dazzling whiteness. Burma's most famous monument is the Golden Pagoda at Rangoon, an important Buddhist sanctuary. The imposing mass of the central building, erected in 1564, rises to a height of about 370 feet and is entirely covered with a thick layer of gold. It contains the only existing relics of the Buddha Sakyamuni, and is the most popular goal of pilgrims from all over Indochina. However, Burmese art has been studied only in a limited way, and to date its historical development is uncertain. In the national heritage a place of particular importance is occupied by manuscripts: these often have lively, rich decorations.

CAMBODIA AND VIETNAM

In the heart of the Indochinese jungle five towers with slender spires dominate the great building of Angkor Vat, a temple of Vishnu that is often called the Cambodian Parthenon because of the perfect harmony of its architectural lines and sculptural decoration. Following an ancient tradition, many visitors gather there every New Year to give thanks to the god and to admire the rich series of reliefs that adorn its galleries, courtyards and rooms. The temple, built in the twelfth century AD, is the grandest and most complete monument left by the Khmer dynasty, who developed an extraordinarily thriving civilization in Cambodia. Beside it are the ruins of Angkor Thom, the capital of the Khmer kings from 900 to around 1400. The walls of this city also serve as an outer enclosure for its principal sanctuary, the Bayon. Covered completely by the jungle, recent work has now freed the Bayon and fully revealed the superb beauty of its massive towers decorated with four gigantic human faces. The reliefs and statues that adorn the temples, though largely subordinate to the architectural lines of the building, are interesting for their sense of taste, elegance of form and detailed accuracy of execution. The themes illustrated are drawn from the rich mythology of the Buddhist and Hindu religions, which were practised simultaneously in Cambodia. The Buddhist figures all have their eyes lowered, as though absorbed in inner meditation, while their lips are closed and have a faint smile (the typical 'Angkor smile') that seems to reflect the serene detachment of those who have given up all worldly things and aspire only to Nirvana.

East of Siam and Cambodia the Indian-Buddhist influence extended as far as the kingdom of Champa, which arose in the second century on the east coast of Annam. The art of Champa (Cham) was at first strongly influenced by the Indian Gupta style, but later it moved away from the elaborate Indian prototypes. The faces of the statues of Dong-duong and Binh-dinh, with their swollen lips, flattened noses and protruding eyebrows, reveal their local origin.

The art of all the countries we have reviewed so far reveals more or less direct Indian inspiration. The influence of Chinese art predominates in north

Vietnam, which became a province under the Han dynasty at the end of the third century BC and remained under Chinese domination until the tenth century AD. Once it achieved independence, Vietnam resisted the attempts at reconquest by the Chinese Sung dynasties and the Mongols, but its art did not escape the typical Chinese taste that had governed it for a thousand years.

INDONESIA

A happy compromise between Indian and local elements also occurred in Indonesia, where the fortunes of the Buddhist religion were strictly tied to the fortunes of the powerful local dynasties. The first Buddhist kingdom arose in the island of Sumatra, and in Java and Bali a civilization known as Indo-Javanese flourished after AD 400.

The most characteristic expression of Indo-Javanese architecture was the *tjandi*, which served both as a place of worship and a burial monument. The cult of ancestor worship had deep roots in Indonesia.

The Indo-Javanese civilization extended to the island of Bali, which was joined to the larger island by political, commercial and sometimes dynastic ties. World-famous for its natural beauty and sacred dances, Bali is also known for its *ille*, temples decorated with flamboyant sculptures that in the course of the centuries have been transformed into a tumult of flowers, leaves, demons and deities.

CHRONOLOGICAL TABLE

3000 BC – *c*. 1400 BC: Culture of Mohenjo-daro and
          Harappa
1400 BC – *c*. 800 BC: Aryan invasion
323 BC – 185 BC: Reign of the Maurya
185 BC – 30 BC: Sunga and Kanva dynasties
:2nd century BC – 1st/2nd century AD: The
          Satavahana in the Deccan
2nd – 4th century AD: Foreign invasions of India
AD 320 – 530: Gupta empire
530–750: Post-Gupta dynasties (the Pandya,
          Chalukya and Pallava)
8th–14th century: India is divided in kingdoms:
    in the North: Kingdom of the Palas 765–1140
          The Senas 1140–1280
          The Pratiharas 8th–10th century
    in Central India:
          The Chandellas 831–1308
          The Rashtrakutas 753–974
          The Chalukyas 973–1200
    in the South:
          The Cholas 864–1279
          The Pandyas 1238–1323
13th–14th century: Sultanate of Delhi
14th–16th century: Hindu revival (1565: fall of the
          Vijayanagar, the last Hindu kingdom)
1526–1857: Moghul empire
1857–   Modern period

BIBLIOGRAPHY

M. DIMAND, Indian Miniatures, New York 1967
H. GOETZ, Art of India, New York
A. LIPPE, Art of India : Stone Sculpture, New York 1962
H. G. RAWLINSON, India : A Short Cultural History,
New York 1952
P. RAWSON, Indian Sculpture, New York
B. ROWLAND, The Art and Architecture of India,
London 1956
R. E. M. WHEELER, Early India and Pakistan,
London 1959

INDEX OF ILLUSTRATIONS

Page 10 Indus Valley art: Large jar. National Museum, New Delhi

11 Indus Valley art: Seal with bull, National Museum, Karachi

12–13 Indian art (Mauryan period): Statuette of the Mother Goddess. Prince of Wales Museum, Bombay

15 Indian art (Mauryan period): Capital of an Asoka column. Museum of Indian art, Calcutta

16 Indian art (Sunga period): Detail of the railing of the Stupa of Bharhut. Museum of Indian Art, Calcutta

17 Indian art (Sunga period): Detail of the railing of the Stupa of Bharhut. Museum of Indian Art, Calcutta

18 Indian art (Sunga period): The railing of the Stupa of Bharhut. Museum of Indian Art, Calcutta

21 Indian art (Sunga period): Bust of a yakshi from Bharhut. Museum of Fine Arts, Boston

22 Indian art (Satavahana period): Details of the North and West gates of Stupa No. 1 at Sanchi

23 Indian art (Satavahana period): Detail of the East gate of Stupa No. 1 at Sanchi

24–5 Indian art (Sunga period): View at Sanchi of Stupa No. 1 or the Great Stupa, and Stupa No. 3

26 Indian art (Sunga period): Stupa No. 3 at Sanchi

29 Indian art (Satavahana period): Relief from the cave-temple at Karle

30 Indian art (Satavahana period): The cave-temple at Karle

31 Indian art (Satavahana period): Entrance to the cave-temple at Bhaja, near Bombay

32 Indian art (Satavahana period): Marble reliefs. British Museum, London

33 Indian art (Satavahana period): Carved panel showing the Stupa of Amaravati. British Museum, London

34 Indian art (Satavahana period): Reliefs from the Stupa of Amaravati (*Above*) National Museum, Madras. (*Below*) British Museum, London

36 Indian art (school of Gandhara): Fragment of a seal. National Museum, Karachi

37 Indian art (school of Gandhara): Head of Bodhisattva. National Museum, Karachi

39 Indian art (Satavahana period): Two young girls. Musée Guimet, Paris

40–1 Indian art (Kushan period): Small stupa. Museum of Indian Art, Calcutta

155

Page 42–3 Indian Art (school of Gandhara): Scene from the life of Buddha. Freer Gallery of Art, Washington, DC.

44 Indian art (school of Mathura): Group of bacchante. National Museum, New Delhi

46 Indian art (school of Gandhara): Female figure. National Museum, Karachi

47 Indian art (school of Gandhara): Head of Bodhisattva. Musée Guimet, Paris

47 Indian art: Stone head with ram's horns. Curzon Museum, Mathura

49 Indian art (school of Mathura): Figure of a dancing yakshi. Victoria and Albert Museum, London

50 Indian art (Gupta period): Buddha. Prince of Wales Museum, Bombay

51 Indian art (Gupta period): Bodhisattva Padmapani. Prince of Wales Museum, Bombay

54 Indian art (Gupta period): Head of Buddha. Curzon Museum, Mathura

55 Indian art (Gupta period): Relief of couple. Curzon Museum, Mathura

56–7 Indian art: General view of the caves of Ajanta

58–9 Indian art (Gupta period): Detail of the façade of Chaitya No. 19. Caves of Ajanta

61 Indian art (Gupta period): Part of the façade of Chaitya No. 19. Caves of Ajanta

62 Indian art (Gupta period): Interior of Chaitya No. 26. Caves of Ajanta

66 Indian art (post-Gupta dynasty): Hindu temple at Citorgarh

67 Indian art (Gupta period): Temple of Mahabodhi at Bodh-Gaya

68 Indian art: *Apsara*, fresco outside Vihara No. 17. Caves of Ajanta

69 Indian art: *Palace scene,* from Vihara No. 1. Caves of Ajanta

71 Indian art: *Buddha preaching among the women*, from Vihara No. 1. Caves of Ajanta

72–3 Indian art: Scene from the *Visvantara jataka*. Caves of Ajanta.

75 Indian art (Chalukya period): (*Above*) Façade of Chaitya No. 10. (*Below*) Reliefs from Sanctuary No. 21. Caves of Ellora

76 Indian art (Pallava period): Monolithic Temple of Bhima, Mamallapuram

77 Indian art (Pallava period): Shore temple, Mamallapuram

Page 78 Indian art (Chalukya period): Vishnu sleeping on a coiled serpent. Prince of Wales Museum, Bombay

79 Indian art (Chalukya period): Hermaphrodite Shiva, relief in the cave of Elephanta near Bombay

80 Indian art (Pallava period): Hindu temple, Nattalamai

83 Indian art (Sena period): Mother and child. Museum of Indian Art, Calcutta

84 Indian art (Medieval period): Stele with figure of Trivikrama. Museum of Indian Art, Calcutta

85 Indian art (Pala or Sena period): Stele with figure of Vishnu. Metropolitan Museum of Art, New York

87 Indian art (Pratihara period): (Left) Tara. National Museum, New Delhi. (Right) Ashtabhuja Marichi. Museum of Indian Art, Calcutta

88 Indian art (Medieval period): Interior of Jain temple at Dilvara, Mount Abu

90–1 Indian art (Rashtrakuta period): Kailasa temple at Ellora.

92–3 Indian art (Chola dynasty): Central sanctuary of the Brihadisvara, Tanjore

95 Indian art (Pandya period): North portal of the Temple of Shiva Nataraja, Cidambaram

96 Indian art (Medieval period): Wheel of the sun-chariot, Konarak

99 Indian art (Chola dynasty): Shiva Nataraja. National Museum, New Delhi

100 Indian art (Moslem period): The Qutb al-Minar, Delhi

101 Indian art (Moslem period): Remains of the Quwwat al-Islam Mosque, Delhi

102 Indian art (Moslem period): The Great Mosque at Ajmer

103 Indian art (Moslem period): Mausoleum of Isa Khan, Delhi

105 Indian art (Hindu revival period): *The toilet of Radha Rajput Pahari*. Freer Gallery of Art, Washington, DC.

106 Indian art (Moslem period): *Young man intent on reading*. Freer Gallery of Art, Washington, DC.

108–9 Indian art (Hindu revival period): General view of the monuments of Ranakpur and the Jain temple of Mount Abu

110–1 Indian art (Hindu revival period): Cloister of the Ramesvaram Temple

112 Indian art (Hindu revival period): Pillars of the *mandapa* of Srirangam Temple

113 Indian art (Hindu revival period): *Gopuras* or portals of Srirangam Temple

157

114 Indian art (Moghul period): The Taj Mahal, Agra
115 Indian art (Moghul period): The Old Palace of Amber
117 Indian art (Moghul period): The Diwan-i hass in the
    Red Fort, Delhi
119 Indian art (Moghul period): *Adoration of Krishna in the
    golden city*. Freer Gallery of Art, Washington, DC.
120–1 Indian art (Moghul period): *Mardkank Khatni bring the
    ring to Maltas, the prison warder*. Freer Gallery of Art,
    Washington, DC.
123 Singhalese art: *Heavenly nymph*, from Sigiriya
123 Singhalese art: Dagoba of Kiri Vehera, Polonnaruva
124 Afghan art: *Spirit of the flowers*. Musée Guimet, Paris
125 Singhalese art: Seated Buddha, Polonnaruva
127 Nepalese art: Figure of Bodhisattva Manjusri. Museum
    of Indian Art, Calcutta
128 Nepalese art: Temple at Bhaktapur
129 Nepalese art: Stupa of Sambhunath, near Katmandu
131 Nepalese art: *Birth of Buddha*. Museum of Indian Art,
    Calcutta
133 Tibetan art: Banner. Musée Guimet, Paris
134 Siamese art: Figure of Buddha. Musée Guimet, Paris
135 Siamese art: Head of Buddha. Staatliches Museum für
    Völkerkunde, Munich
136 Siamese art: Interior courtyard of the Vat Phra Keo,
    Bangkok
138–9 Siamese art: *A Buddhist paradise*. Musée Guimet, Paris
140 Khmer art: Apsaras, from a relief at Angkor Vat
141 Khmer art: Figure of Tara. Musée Guimet, Paris
142 Cham art: Figure of Lokesvara. Musée Guimet, Paris
143 Cham art: Makara dragon. Musée Guimet, Paris
145 Indonesian (Bali) art: *The goddess and the monster*.
    Koninklijk Instituut voor de Tropen, Amsterdam
146 Laotian art: Figure of Buddha. Musée Guimet, Paris